SELECTED POEMS

Jeremy Gadd grew up in Armidale, New South Wales. After graduating from the National Institute of Dramatic Art, he worked extensively in professional theatre in Australia and the United Kingdom before concentrating on his writing, which includes plays, the publication of novels and short stories as well as poetry. He has also written dialogue for a dance performed by The Sydney Dance Company at the Opera House and he collaborated on one of the first livre d' artistes to be produced in the United Kingdom since William Morris, a work that is now in rare book collections. He later earned Master of Arts with Honours and PhD degrees from the University of New England and is a Writing Fellow of the Fellowship of Australian Writers (NSW).

SELECTED POEMS

JEREMY GADD

ARCADIA

First published 2013 by Arcadia,
the general books' imprint of
Australian Scholarly Publishing,
7 Lt Lothian St North
North Melbourne Victoria 3051

TEL 03+93296963
FAX 03+93295452
aspic@ozemail.com.au
www.scholarly.info

ISBN 978-1-925003-29-1

Cover design and typesetting *Sarah Anderson*
Printing and Binding *Tenderprint Pty Ltd*

CONTENTS

ACKNOWLEDGEMENTS

The author would like to thank the editors of the literary magazines, newspapers, periodicals and anthologies in which these poems were first published:

In Australia

The Sydney Morning Herald, The Australian, The West Australian, The Newcastle Herald, Australian Writer, Nation Review, Mattoid, Blast, Social Alternatives, Spindrift, Northern Perspective, Eidolon, The Bondi View, Hermes, Consciousness, Writers Voice, FreeXpresSion, A Sporting Declaration (an anthology published by Phoenix Publications), *Idiom 23°, The Rainbow Argus, The Lyre-Bird Monthly, The Daily Planet, The Australian Music Teacher Magazine, Wildlife News, Shades of Happiness* (an anthology published by Holt, Rinehart and Winston), *Australian Better Gardens and Home Ideas, Hobo, P(philosophy) A(activism) N(nature), Positive Words, Whisper to the Moon* (an anthology published by Rutter Publications), *The Astrological Monthly Review, Arts Rush* and *The Artist's Chronicle*

In the USA

The Conservative Review, Paisley Moon, Poetry Break, Phase & Cycle, Manna, Parnassus, Mobius, Art Times, Xenophilia, Pirate Writings, Dream International Quarterly, Aboriginal Science Fiction, The Poetic Knight, The Eloquent Athiest and *Epic Journal*

In the UK

Resurgence, Poetry Wales, Eternal Words (an anthology published by Poetry Now), *The Swansea Review, Together, Orbis, Staple* 36, *Poetry Monthly, Poetrymonthly.com, International Poets* (an anthology published by Arrival Press), *Poetry and Audience, Candelabrum, Target, Spokes* (Issues 7, 27 & 29–30), *Words Worth, Tears in the Fence, Firing Squad, Dream Catcher, Christian Messenger* (an anthology published by Triumph House) and *Weyfarers* 113

Elsewhere

Poetry Salzburg Review (Austria) and the *Journal of Australian Literature* (India).

TO ALL THOSE TORMENTED SOULS

To all those tormented souls striving
for political power or artistic immortality;
to all those ambitious to make their mark
on society or posterity, who accept stress
as part of the price they must pay:
the politicians, fearful of some secret aspect
of their past being paraded in public;
the writers, scratching at old wounds for inspiration –
does it justify the angst and the anguish?
Surely, no degree of fame or reverential
whispering of your name can atone
for families forgotten, for time forfeited;
for lives squandered in the chase to achieve
what must ultimately prove ephemeral?

I WATCH THE COFFEE COLOURED DAY

I watch the coffee coloured day
                    spill milk bright,
counting spoonfuls heaped with once life
                    into the cloistered clay.
O – why white flowers at funerals?

A careening crow caroused with my cross
                    murmuring sympathy
for the lost. Toll'd my dirge
                    in cawing clangs.
O – why bitumen black for the bearers?

Gravel my grave in morning glory
                    or the word wormed
leaves of a cheerful story
                    to warm my barren breast.
O – cover my heart in colours.

AND IF SOME TIME THE SATELLITES

And if some time the satellites of your charm
revolve around another sphere,
don't mention me in your memoirs,
among the moods and the men that have passed;
don't decorate your dinners, give laurels to your winners,
and speak of me with your next breath:
don't sully the memory of our love,
of what was a grail, by displaying the mirror
of our madness; the deed reflects more upon you.
Mention me most in your mind's quiet moments,
murmur my name to the Keeper of the Cross,
ask him to lead me out of this dark,
for silent are the songs of the suffering waters,
and silver the tears of the silent stars

LIFE

(according to Pete the
professional sea-worm seller)

Here we are, you and I,
 two carbon based bipeds
suspended by our feet
from the southern hemisphere
of a rotating lump of cooling
molten magma (due to
some intangible force called
gravity), while orbiting
a dying yellow star
and simultaneously hurtling
through an infinite frozen
vacuum at terrifying speed,
hoping like hell we don't
collide with debris from
disintegrated celestial structures
such as asteroids, comets,
spiral nebulas and planetoids –
and now you tell me
there is nowhere to park?

WITHIN MY WEATHERED WALLS

Within my weathered walls two forces fume
and force their will. One leans to light,
one shadow clings and tempts my tongue
                with titbits on strings.

Within this same frame serenes some force
blind to the burden of beasthood and bone
who expects me to winnow sin from my saint,
                salt from my sea.

I am no Mammon or nail-bitten Messiah,
nor sinlit sow's son or merely molecules
but a man shroud-bound and tailored by Fate,
                measure me in minutes.

Wide-eyed through a welter of darkness
I wend through that thimbleworth of world
that is mine, threading toward the long light,
                heavy with humus.

ON READING A LETTER

The falling leaves beat like drums,
a muffled welcome, this Autumn,
to a boy born far away, my
brother's first, proud words proclaim;
to their tattoo my thoughts of you
march past in the morning light.
O give him sight to see such things
as speckled spots an sparrows' wings,
the shining eyes his being brings;
let him learn to love the longest grief,
let him not condemn the thief,
give him ears to hear such sounds
as dew drops bursting on the ground,
the magic melodies of Spring, 0
give him sight to see such things.
Give him tongues to taste the thrill
of reaching the impossible;
lend him lips to sip the sight
of Dawn, resplendent in its light,
of flitting bats before the night
draws blinds upon the day –

And when grass blades beneath his feet
parry with the Winter sleet,
and leaves that blow across his path
remind him life, like leaves, won't last,
that what is green and stretched in joy
turns brown and withers like the toy
discarded by the growing boy,
and he is drowned in dread,
have no regrets that boughs are bare,
sing like a sun that you were there.
O give him sight to see such things.

SO, SUCCESS APPEARS
TO HAVE PASSED YOU BY

So, success appears to have passed you by,
leaving you behind and covered in dust
like a hitch-hiker left beside the road;
and now you've decided to denigrate
the ways of the world as unjust.
Whatever led you to believe you are owed?
Who told you life would be fair?
It is up to you to accept and adjust.
So, realising you might always be
a lesser poet playing in a minor key,
and recognising, in the end, all is futility,
be grateful you still have your senses
and the ability to see and smell
the fragrant gardenia at your lapel.

ON FINGAL HEAD

There is a headland near my home
where jagged black, basalt blocks
face the sea and, for fifty
sheer feet, fall vertically.
Where masochistic waves beat
with relentless regularity
against the volcanic rocks.
The spray that is formed
from the shock, like front
row forwards in a final,
floats far inland; coating
the fronds of the pandanus palms,
precariously clinging to the crevices
between the water-worn rocks,
with an encrustation of salt.
It is one of Nature's unique places,
where the inverted basin of the sky,
horizon, hinterland and sea,
fuse in inspirational majesty.
Although not as predictable
as lunar driven tides,
I frequently wander that hillside,
breathing ozone invigorated air
and soaking in its atmosphere.
Recently, I went there for a walk,
but weighed down with suburban blues
and worries of impending rates and dues,
hardly heard the crashing surf
or the cries of the terns and other
birds hang-gliding over my head.
I stood despondent and depressed,

unresponsive to all about me.
Even oblivious to the way fine
droplets of water from the spray
created hundreds of iridescent
rainbows, far across the bay.
And for the first and only time
contemplated suicide –
until I became aware,
I wasn't the only one standing there.
In silhouette against the sky
stood a man wearing a suit and tie
and carrying a bulging briefcase.
Another tourist I assumed,
of the type who look and leave
with photos of what they failed
to see – but he was different.
Lowering his briefcase to the grass
he held his hands out before him
as if asking for alms then,
bending his body into the wind,
and trusting the gusts to hold him,
he stepped off the precipice –
and hung suspended in the air!
Astounded I could only stare
as he invited me to join him
in mid-air, while down below
the foam licked the rocks,
like savage animals licking
their chops in hungry anticipation.
I'm sure it wasn't my imagination.
Even though I know it sounds
absurd, I swear I heard as
clear as a bird, a single resonating
note, eerily echoing around me.
Although cold enough to cause
a shiver, the sound made
the air quiver, like heat haze

on a sweltering day; and through
a series of rips in the cosmic fabric,
dozens of beckoning hands appeared,
enticing me to walk on air.
But in the quagmire of my emotions
something started to stir
and, looking into the abyss below,
I understood that the difference
between a rut and a grave is its depth,
and I decided not to let go.
I shook my head saying
'I'm staying … I'm staying'.
The note built to a crescendo
and, like a swaying sea of weed,
the phantom hands beckoned me
with an increasing intensity.
The furious wind nearly succeeded
in sucking me over the cliff.
Then diminuendo – the mystical
man straightened his tie,
nodded goodbye and was gone.
And all this while the sun shone!
Once more I heard the sound
of the surf, and might have thought
nothing had occurred – except
for the briefcase on the ground.
I continue to wander that wind
exposed hill, and find for all
its noisy waves and quarrelling
terns, an inner serenity there.
And if there is a moral to this
verse, it is take a taxi
and avoid the hearse.
It was only later I happened
to find the forgotten briefcase
Death left behind, and its
list of names, including mine.

THE THERAPEUTIC VALUE OF TREES

Trees grow more precious
                    in the city.
In the country, their numbers
                    and abundance
rarely entice a second glance,
                    unlike trees
struggling for survival among
                    concrete and fumes,
like those growing from
                    traffic islands
or those in back streets,
                    nurtured to provide
shade for cafe society and relief
                    from the
omnipresence of bricks and mortar.
                    Even the
gnarled shapes of their trunks
                    provide healing
balm for architecturally
                    tired eyes
and battered egos and psyches;
                    revealing nature
as an Hippocrates of the spirit,
                    soothing mind sores,
succouring souls with foliage
                    and the beauty
of their tortured, tough bark.

AWARE OF THE BONE
BENEATH THE SKIN

Aware of the bone beneath the skin
I set out to seek the most precious
of all the multiplicity of things
that lie in limbo, fly above,
swim beneath, crawl or walk
upon this astounding world:
only to find the most valuable,
rarer than gold or myrrh,
or infinitely carated diamonds;
dearer than a mother's delight
in her child; is that with which
we are all born rich in –
but die beggared and bereft of,
like a worked out mine – time.

IN OUR MONEY OBSESSED

In our money obsessed consumer society
there are affluent high-flyers on Easy Street,
a thrifty and frugal bourgeoisie
and those unable to make ends meet.
There are big spenders of munificent prodigality
and misers who skimp and save,
there are the needy, enmeshed in their penury
and the destitute, unable to even pay for their graves;
but none are so poor as the poor in spirit.
Whether on welfare, bureaucrat or lawyer,
tradesman, banker or chauffeur,
no amount of re-mortgaging, hand-outs
or help will alleviate their poverty.

FROM A BULL-NOSED
IRON VERANDAH

I

Civilisations rise and crumble like cake;
their destinies, their survival or fall
as unpredictable as a child's bouncing ball,
determined by earthquakes and random events.
From damp Stonehenge to arid Giza,
from Lake Titicaca to Angkor Wat
stand statues, temples and mausoleums,
remnants of societies long overcome.
From the scorched columns of Persepolis
to the debris on Athens' acropolis,
their ruins litter continents like refuse
left behind by untidy picnickers.

II

Aborigines did not bother with buildings,
and despite – or perhaps because of
having travelled wide and far
from this bull-nosed iron verandah –
beneath which we are listening
to the baas of new born lambs
and watching ibis strut and file
along the billabong, as they do by the Nile –
my marvelling eyes are being drawn
to a blooming mauve jacaranda tree,
which is much more impressive to me
than any man-made building or
sculpture of Apollo or Ra could ever be

and, unexpectedly, I understand
the indigenous Australians' reticence.
Unlike the awesome constructions
of ancient emperors, architects
and engineers, the jacaranda's beauty
can provoke a tear and its blossom
will be renewed at this time every year.

ODE TO PINDAR

Pindar's poems praise the winners
of antiquity's sacred games,
when those most favoured by the gods
won wreathes of wild celery
or of leaves from laurel and olive trees,
or garlands of Dorian parsley
and widespread prestige and fame
and, for a moment, became more than men.

Beautiful of body and, originally, amateur,
their beards often as soft as gossamer,
Pindar's panegyrics lauded
the virile, physical achievers
with celebratory verses – and prayers
that they retain their modesty,
for nothing was so unbecoming
to a Greek as self-centred vanity.

Not interested in extolling kings like Creon,
Pindar sang about Xenophon of Korinth,
winner of the foot race and pentathlon,
and the veteran, Chromios of Aitna,
winner of the chariots' first place;
about a boy boxer who stood against all-comers,
and Hegesias, winner with the mule-car –
and his words carried their glory afar.

Now a country unimagined
by those who lived in classical times,
will host the year Two Thousand's
modern Olympic games
and a new list of names will be
added to the roll-call of repute,
and reputations lost as well as made,
as they were so long ago
in the Peloponnesian peninsular's shady glades.
What would Pindar say to you,
the athletes competing for gold medals?
'Conduct yourselves with valor and virtue'?
And, if victorious, like Cato repeatedly
finishing his speeches to the Roman senate
with the statement: 'Carthage must be destroyed',
perhaps his muse will whisper in your ear,
'remember you are mortal and destined for a funeral bier'.

NOT SINCE WADING IN THE WATERS

Not since wading in the waters of the womb,
has the illuminative truth, extracted like a tooth,
ached so loudly in the mouth of my mind:
without the bitter wind blows no sweet;
that passion is paltry, more fickle than fate,
love is learnt through loss and healing hate.
That the kiss of the coin reeks of bad breath,
and the sweet implements tooth decay.
Melt me a minute, I'll show you wasted hours.
sacrifice lambs, I'll show you dead sheep.
In the wardrobe of woe hangs a happy coat,
every waking points the path to sleep.
These are the truths that bind us all.
So I jump for joy, knowing Death will call.

NEXT TIME WE WILL MEET

Next time we will meet where the black crows fly
backwards to shade the sun from their eyes;
where the wallabies wash their weary feet
in mirages that shimmer in the desert heat.
I will wait by the dam that never dries,
where the women of the tribe sing their lullabies
and listen, with the old men, to the 'Lost Friend's Lament'.
The date doesn't matter though
the swag of years grows fatter:
If you lose your way, don't risk the day,
travel by night by the moon's cool light,
the Southern Cross will steer you right.
If need be I will wait for ever and ever,
though next we may meet in the Never, Never.

MANKIND IS MADE

Mankind is made of immortal music:
our songs are recorded by the planets;
our voices sing harmony with the stars,
yet we wither like words left unsaid.
Halfway to heaven, worms wear at our feet,
we would avoid fire, but enjoy the heat;
like shadows that shrink before the rising sun,
our days diminish, our web is soon spun.
Yet, amid the cacophony of our cares
and contradictions, we find symphonies
of silence and pauses of perfection.
A blind man's burden makes senses increase,
the approaching chill increases the fleece.

CARL SAGAN SAYS

Carl Sagan says the first television
signals broadcast on Earth are still
oscillating out into space, and that
they will continue to do so for
infinity ...

             Donald Duck cartoons
and Rawhide, the Bay of Pigs fiasco
and the Cuban crisis, advertisements
for detergents and cheap ties passing
Alpha Centauri at the speed of light
and on and on into the abyss of time ...

             But television transmissions
are simply pulses of electricity and thoughts
are also believed to be electrochemical
sparks, flashing between the neurons of
our brains ...

             If long forgotten
television series can ghoulishly continue
to exist in the ether, waiting to be watched
by alien recipients, why not human
thoughts too ?

             If so, then surely every
thought ever thought still persists, and
in the year three thousand and thirty five
someone or some thing will be receiving
this live ...

ACROSS THE VALLEY

Across the valley, as far as I can see,
over the top of a sea of trees, there are
eucalyptus leaves shimmering in the sunlight,
like shoals of minnows shining in shallow water.
A gap in the leafy canopy indicates
where a great forest giant has died.
There, where a healthy gum once elbowed
its neighbours for room to breathe,
whenever wind bent its boughs with a mighty heave,
stands the gaunt skeleton of a dead tree.
Its brittle branches break and fall
and its white trunk rots where
it once stood tall but, near its base –
I'm sure – green shoots await the next rainfall.

REFLECTIONS ON YOUTH

I

It is noon, and gazing north from
my rented room, along the arc of
Bondi's famous esplanade and beach,
towards the outcrop of rock locally
known as Ben Buckler, shimmering
in the heat haze beneath a topless sky,
the yellow sand spreads like molten
butter, into the surf, as if on rye.

II

Customers saunter in and out of cafes
in a steady lunch-time trade
while giggling girls play tip-and-run
as they flirt with boys in the shade.
Brown, young, swim-suited bodies –
and some which are not so nubile –
are sprawled on their Technicolor towels,
as though posing for a Ken Done painting
or, for the more morbidly minded,
laid out like cadavers on
multi-coloured mortuary slabs.

III

Even the sunshine seems slothful.
The holiday-makers – and those who simply
have time to kill on their hands –
are aimlessly wandering; window shopping,
feeding sea-gulls; a surfeit of indolence
that prompts pondering on the adage
'youth is wasted on the young'.

IV

In the late afternoon, the sinking sun's rays
strike the windows of the apartment buildings
and deflect onto the sea, causing reflections
to bob about like globules of mercury on the water.
Then, as Sol sets behind huge banks of billowing
cloud, the panes of glass flash orange fire,
burning buildings in an orgy of imaginary mass destruction …

V

Night has now cast its cloak along the shore
and the lights of the Telecom telephone booth
domes are glowing like lit coals in a grate.
Fairy lights outline the silhouette of the tower
of the Bondi Hotel and the headlights of cars
search along Campbell Parade as, like whores
winking back at them, traffic lights blink red.

In the street below, buses' air-brakes hiss
as they stop to let off workers on their
way home – and the sudden wail of an
ambulance siren, demanding right of way,
sends a chill down the length of my spine.

VI

And I decide: youth isn't wasted on the young.
It is a gift, given to those in their physical
prime while they still believe they are immortal;
while the vagaries of aging are still merely mythology;
so that young years can be enjoyed without glancing
over shoulders at lengthening shadows …

HISTORY AND LEGENDS
RECORD THE NAMES

History and legends record the names
of the renowned and those who fell from grace:
Alcibiades, who was banished to the Hellespont;
handsome Hector, who fell out of favour
with the gods and met his death
in the dust by the Dardanian Gates;
poor Daedalus, who dared to fly too high
and fell with his son to their fate;
but what of the innumerable unrecorded
names who aspired to their place in the sun,
only to find themselves in the shade,
finished before they had begun?
Not everyone finds success; like Sisyphus,
some of us are destined to roll stones.

ORACLES, SEERS
AND SOOTHSAYERS

Poor Cassandra predicted gloom,
and everyone wished Agamemnon
had left her behind at her loom.

Clairvoyant Cassandra foresaw
the ruin of the House of Atreus,
and in foretelling the future
found foresight a minus not a plus.

Poor Cassandra, prophetess of gloom,
lived to regret leaving her mother's womb,
for gifted Cassandra learned too late,
telling the truth as you see it
often inspires hostility and hate.

Oracles, seers and soothsayers
are destined to be denigrated
if the future of which they speak
is ominous or bleak.

Like ostriches putting their heads
in the sand, people prefer not to know
that, tomorrow, ill-omened winds might blow.

Think kindly of Cassandra,
she spoke out of honesty not pique.

AFTER WATCHING A PROGRAMME ON THE LIFE OF RICHARD BURTON

So what is left, when it is said and done,
and you are looking down the barrel
of the smoking gun of old age,
disease or another of Death's agents –
cigarettes, pesticides and high
voltage power lines – that prey upon
the frail physical frame of the human case?
An easy trip into the waiting grave?
A hasty reckoning of what was
received against what you gave?
A glimpse into what might have been?
A sudden insight into what it all means?
That a fiercely lived life can be a
tranquilliser for those afraid of the dark?

BEFORE IT BECOMES TOO LATE

Before it becomes too late,
and hate begets hate,
the wounds and cuts caused by
those prepared to hack at the whole,
to dismember and isolate,
in order to divide and rule the state,
have to be treated and healed.
If hot tempers are to cool
and injuries resulting from nepotism,
political correctness and secret deals
are not to leave permanent weals
and scars on the national psyche,
it has to be clearly understood
governments must govern for the common good.

HEAVEN IS

Heaven is in the caress of a breeze
rustling wind shredded banana leaves
and bringing relief from the oppressive
heat hanging heavily on the evening air.
It is in the distant rumble of thunder
warning of the approaching storm,
and in the effervescent splashes
of the bright and bloody blooms
of bougainvillaea, frangipani and hibiscus
revealed by the lightning's flashes
and proudly worn like wounds of war
on the lushly green tropical foliage.
Heaven is in the soporific sound
of the massed cicadas' symphony
and in the throbbing song of the frogs,
singing as they sense the rain.
It is in the deafening drumming
on the corrugated iron roof overhead,
and in the sullen, hissing sound
as the drops strike the steaming ground.
It is in the crystal clear atmosphere
left after the downpour has departed.
Heaven is everywhere.

DEAR MONSIEUR BONNARD

To:

Monsieur Bonnard c/- Hayward Gallery

London

1994

Dear Monsieur Bonnard,

We met at your retrospective exhibition, nearly thirty years after you died. I mentioned how much I enjoyed your work but did not catch your reply. You appear to have led a quiet life at Villa du Bosquet, growing old gracefully in an aesthetic and dignified way. I am now writing to express my appreciation for your finesse and thank you for the guided tour of your home – it was well worth the price of admission, despite my ending the day footsore.

The view from *The French Window* was wonderful, as was *The Landscape with the Red Roof* and, gazing at *The Stormy Sea Over Cannes*, I swear raindrops struck the palm of my outstretched hand. *The Walk in the Garden* was inspiring too (except when I tripped on *The Garden Steps* – I feared I'd keep falling until I reached Dieppe!). Don't forget to keep *The Gate* shut and forgive me for calling your dachshund a mutt.

And while I'm apologising, I assure you I did not mean to be rude when I happened to intrude on *Marthe*, your wife, in *The Dining Room*. Elegant in her pale high heels she appeared to be *Preparing For Lunch: A Still Life*. The meal looked such a treat, I wanted to be invited to sit down and eat at *The Long Table Covered in Red Cloth*.

On a hunch I sought you in *The Artist's Studio,* but you must have been out on *The Patio.* The room was so tidy I can only assume your maid was an absolute saint. It might have been gouache or oil paint, but I thought I caught a whiff of perfume. Although I don't regard myself as a prude, I have to admit I felt a voyeur when, looking through an open door, I saw someone *Nude in the Bathtub.*

I found you, finally, in *The Pencil Self Portrait on Paper,* (and similar studies) owlishly staring at me through round austere spectacles; your face pensive and pinched with concentration as you scrutinized your reflection in a mirror; engrossed with minutiae, creating art from the mundane and everyday; concerned with actuality – with what is substantial – not fantasy.

I admired your composition and superb technique; some paintings gave me a glow I attributed to your exquisite use of burnt sienna and cadmium yellow; other impressions left me unable to speak, the images so real I could almost feel paving stones under my feet … but the pièce de résistance was, for me, what is reputed to have been your last painting – the beautiful *Blossoming Almond Tree* – which I saw as a motif of renewal.

According to the catalogue, you died on 23rd January.

Was it blossom painted the previous thaw or the following spring you never saw?

If the latter, for such a realist, it was a vast leap of imagination – your ultimate act of creation.

Yours sincerely,

Jeremy Gadd

BUTTERFLY

The beauty of a butterfly
isn't only to be found
in its iridescent colours
or in the delicateness of its
fragile wings but also in
the freedom its fluttering
brings.

LITTLE LOUIS

Because his mother was
never home
little Louis left-alone
thought his mother was
a telephone.

EDUCATION

Education consists of learning
a lot of facts
we did not realise we needed
to know and which
we later delude ourselves we
knew all the time.

MISSED OPPORTUNITY

I

Early Portuguese, Dutch, French and,
possibly Spanish seafarers, were familiar
with the barren and ship-threatening
coast of Western Australia;
from Albany to the rugged, red-rouged
cliffs of sunbathed Broome and beyond Derby
it was marked on their charts as Terra Incognita
and used as a navigational guide:
on sighting its smoke-smudged shoreline
mariners swung helms until bows pointed north-
north-east, towards the exotic Spice Islands.
Profit foremost in their minds they had no
interest in a parched, inhospitable wilderness.
But the British, cold-shouldered by their
European competitors, decided to sail
south and, on reaching the Roaring Forties,
turned eastwards and discovered lush
grasslands growing in temperate lattitudes;
and there, at Circular Quay,
with the truculent assistance of convict labour,
they founded what became a nation.

II

Now it is said, sotto voce of course,
that the British Establishment's greatest gripe
today is that it exiled the dregs of
its Eighteenth Century society
to what was expected to be a bleak,
dreary existence in a distant uncivilised land –
only to learn, belatedly, that the place
was resource rich, a natural paradise
blessed with a surfeit of sun,
where people could enjoy a life-style second to none.

III

Even if only remotely true there is delicious
irony in the possibility British snobbery
and condescension about things colonial
might be caused by regret or jealousy:
that the Brits rue missing the opportunity
to emigrate, en masse, from Albion's pleasant
but damp, grey and overcrowded islands,
sinking beneath the weight of population and the past,
to a brighter future at Botany Bay.

IT IS A TRUISM

It is a truism that the best things
in life are free; the air we breathe,
the will to achieve, compassion, laughter,
life itself and the natural beauty about us;
found in a zephyr ruffling calm water
or the absent-minded brush of a woman's hand
as she fondly tousles her child's hair.
That everything has its price is a cliché:
for example, the cost of convenient and
comfortable cars is pollution and,
eventually, pollution costs clean air.
But some things are beyond price.
The price of life is one owed death
and sooner or later the debt must be paid

TODAY I SAW A
THOUSAND THINGS

Today I saw a thousand things
you are unable to see:
the Balinese bells you hung on the trees
tickled by the wind sang sombrely:
lilies lay lifeless on the pond
like lessons yet to be learnt:
Abbie tried to catch a goldfish
but, happily, it got away,
a slippery glimmer of gold
and red, surviving for another day.
Our lives were so scorched by your hot will
that while we live you linger still.
I lived today in your memory.
From today you live in me.

NOT FOR US INFINITE EXISTENCE

Not for us infinite existence,
like energy, which can neither be
created or destroyed …
Not for us the immense power
of gravity, which gradually compresses
matter to make the universe we can see
and that awesome amount we cannot.
Not for us the splendid magnificence
of galaxies majestically spinning through time
or the steady orbit of planets sublime;
such is our fragility
that we are akin to shooting stars
which, when viewed from afar,
blaze for a brief moment of glory.

ONE DAY I IMAGINED

One day I imagined I broke the bonds
of gravity that bind our species to this
pleasant but overcrowded blue planet
and, soaring on solar winds, set sail
across interstellar space on a voyage
of exploration into infinity …
Beyond the frozen worlds orbiting
at the outer edge of our sun's system
and past the Great Galaxy in Andromeda,
the visual limit of the known universe,
until I saw myself sitting on a beach,
watching two moons rise in awesome beauty
over a golden sea, and I realised
I had glimpsed our destiny.

THE DEAD DO NOT DREAM

The dead do not dream:
few dreams are found in morgues;
only the living have dreams;
but the dreams of the living
often bring forth the dead,
whether people, aspirations or ideas.

The dead can be brought back to life
by dreams and dreams are supposed to be
a benign form of therapy
when dark corners of suppressed
memories and deliberately forgotten
events and fears are exposed,
letting the relieving light in,
allowing renewal to begin

SHE WAS ONE-EYED

She was one-eyed, metaphorically, in her youth;
of closed mind, intransigent, insensitive,
occasionally uncouth; often unwilling to accept
the truth if it wasn't what she wanted to hear.
In old age she became one-eyed literally but,
nearly blind, saw more clearly and, opening
her mind to the world as easily as if she had
unlocked a door, mellowed, became considerate,
inquisitive and, with each passing year, ironically
acquired wisdom and insight worthy of a sage
or seer until, as her heart finally faltered,
I began to understand the complex
psyche of she who was my mother.
Now I too see that I will miss her terribly.

BONDI BUS

It was obvious he was hungry;
but on a crowded bus from
Bondi to the city he failed to
attract either concern or pity.
It was the way he ate his apple;
oblivious to all about him,
he leant, arm hooked around
a chrome pole for support,
delicately savouring the last
shreds of fruit still clinging
to its browning core.
His half open eyes were glazed;
he was gaunt; his hair closely
cropped and his singlet faded blue.
His young life still to be lived,
he sucked, nibbled and relished
his meagre meal, smacking his lips
like a gourmet appreciating a five
star repast; his pleasure, his rapture,
his appreciation for a small mercy,
the sole indication of his plight.

SAD ARE THE SEA-URCHINS

Sad are the sea-urchins,
for they shall never sing.
Glad are the budgerigars
for the joy their voices bring.
Patient are dumb animals
serenely awaiting their fate;
furrowed are the brows of those
who attend to affairs of state.
Darkest is the sky before dawn
when daylight drenches the earth;
raven black are the undertakers
carrying corpses to the hearse.
Each has its unique place
in this astonishing universe.

WHEN WEIGHED DOWN

When weighed down with the woes
of the world and the contrariness
of corporate affairs, I often
replenish my jaded spirit at
the well of all things natural.
There, in deep satisfying gulps
I quench my thirst, drinking sights,
smells and sounds that, for all our
technical ingenuity, will never be surpassed:
the deafening silence of a balmy night
before thunderstorms cool down the valley;
the calm, mute surface of the river
before a wind whips up waves – finding
sustenance in Nature's constant inconstancy.

THE RIVER

I

For millions of years the river has
wound down from its headwaters
around Mount Warning, carving
a valley through the caldera of
an ancient, extinct, volcano.
Where molten lava once spewed
forth, seeds took root in what
eventually evolved into fertile soil
and, flourishing, grew into primeval
forest; pristine, replete with red cedar
and hoop-pines, bangalow palms,
Moreton Bay fig trees, orchids,
its canopy festooned with vines:
beauty born out of an igneous hell where
thousands of people now toil and dwell.
The tall timbers have long been hewn,
turned into furniture and paper,
the enduring into the ephemeral.
Now even the river is not immune
from the widespread urban assault
population growth has brought.
Houseboats and pleasure craft
speed or patiently plod the waterways;
inquisitive passengers aboard tourist
cruises subject waterfront dwellings
to their curious and, often, envious gaze.

Today, ash falls from the sky again
and, beneath a rain of charred cane,
from fields deliberately set on fire,
the river ambles past a sugar mill
reeking of sickly sweet molasses,
its seasonal smoke plume stark
against the haze and surrounding hills.
In the evenings, the sky glows
(as it must in prehistoric times)
with red reflections of the flames below,
like ethereal forges and furnaces,
as vivid as the petals of azaleas,
as enticing as confectionery.
Where herons and egrets strut
the shores, shoals and shallows
await unwary coxswains, except,
these days, the channels are charted,
tamed by safe water markers and
lateral lights that guide at night.
Nowadays, where sea eagles continue
to soar, houses litter the hillsides,
their windows overlooking
long-necked cormorants as they dive
like meteors through pungent breezes
announcing the presence of a piggery.
But, beneath this rustic, domestic veneer,
something of what was still survives.

II

The river's mouth is marked by a
promontory known as Point Danger.
Renowned for its unsafe entrance
and hazardous reefs offshore, this
outlet to the ocean often altered and
rock was quarried to construct massive,

cyclopean training walls – breakwaters –
in a conceited and eventually futile
attempt to create a deep navigable channel.
The result concentrated the current
until, encountering incoming surf,
it slowed, depositing particles and sand
and, awash with angry white water,
crossing the bar became perilous,
not to be attempted on an ebbing tide.
Unpredictable, and rejecting all attempts
to be confined and restrained,
the river's channels flux and change,
its sandbars constantly shifting.
Seemingly solid banks are undercut
and the river rolls on relentlessly
until it discharges its life-giving
contents into the corrosion causing
salt sea, where even the most solid,
given time, is ultimately consumed
by the brine – there is something
familiar about the fate of the river.
Unlike the ocean that rhythmically
recedes and returns, its tidal influence
felt far upstream, the river only goes
one way; water refuses to flow up hill
and straws afloat on the stream of life
have no alternative other than to go
with the flow – for the river has
a beginning, a middle and an end:
a youth spent rushing headlong from
the hills and a meandering middle age,
eventually reaching its estuary
and becoming one with the sea
like a soul interfacing with eternity …

I AM NO PAUPER TO YOUR TRUST

I am no pauper to your trust
and beg you likewise be to mine,
for every doubt that digs your brow
plants seeds of sorrow down my spine
and, if unweeded, these will grow
and spoil the fruit of every kiss.
Policemen can't foretell the crime
and I can't guarantee that skies
will stay as clear as your sweet eyes
but this I'll promise to all time:
whenever doubt gnaws at your nails
or like a cloud hangs over roof,
then shall this rhyme, a sunny feature,
shine through to you in perfect proof.

ON BELLEVUE HILL

Feeling overcast and grey like the weather,
I trudge, tired of city life and of swallowing
bitter pills, wet and dejected up Bellevue Hill,
the harbour dull molten metal to my left,
undulating ocean to my right.
Matching my melancholy mood,
doleful clouds accumulate and coalesce
to form a leaden-hued layer above me
and the moist, glistening, red tiled
roofs of the constantly expanding suburbs.
Squalls sweep along the eastern horizon,
their dark columns a colonnade
connecting the dome of the sky to the sea.
Leaves, like flags too tired to wave
or without a cause worth unfurling for,
hang languidly in the oppressive humidity.
It feels as if all is in abeyance;
as though Time has tired of the enormity
of its task and paused to rest and recuperate.
Drizzle drifts and is caught in the net
of my hair and, as a waterspout briefly
towers offshore, I look out over
the raindrop bejewelled undergrowth,
at the damp, dark-barked and
rain-wreathed dripping trees and,
listening to the distant warbling call
of a currawong, feel, for an
overwhelming fraction of a second,
privileged, grateful and humble to have
experienced this inspirational view I see –
this minuscule moment in eternity.

PROPHECY 452 A.D.

The consummate politician, in a democracy,
is one who survives in perpetuity,
but to hold on to power, legally,
requires continual electoral support:
an unlikely event; therefore politicians
offer smorgasbords of policies
to every pressure group they want to please,
and what the Haves have to the Have Nots;
and tragedy becomes inevitable.
The barbarians gather at the gates;
the forces of greed and jealousy,
ready and willing to ravage and hate,
to take what they cannot create,
and the demagogue carries the key

THERE'S AN ANGEL

There's an angel for every drop of rain,
as many angels as there are kernels of grain.
There are angels for uppers - and for lows,
angels behind the briefest rainbows.
Guardian angels hover over the innocent
(there are even angels for those who are bent).
There are angels for those in distress or lost,
an angel for every soul who perished in the Holocaust.
Like flights of birds seeking their nests at evening,
the world is noisy with their wings' beating.
But if the number of angels that fit on a pin
is so numerous it makes the mind reel and spin,
why did you have to join them too?
Surely there are enough without you?

BRITISH CLASS

I

The British are obsessed with class:
from lower to upper with sundry
strata in between, including
an unemployed underclass,
working, middle, a chattering class,
aristocracy, drones and a queen –
not only do they categorise
their citizenry like an apiary
but, in keeping with their etiquette,
whenever you buy a train ticket
or purchase a postage stamp,
you are automatically asked:
'First or Second class?'
Their preoccupation borders on farce.

II

No wonder the cool climated British
felt at home in India's heat –
the social system was de rigueur
and, from omnipotent Rajah
to impoverished untouchables
in the bazaar, the sahibs
were treated as elite ...

III

Why the urge to put people in boxes?
It is one of those paradoxes.
According to *The Concise Oxford Dictionary*
to stereotype is to formalise –
'to impart monotonous regularity'.
But why want to negate individuality
– unless to keep the lid on a restless society?
Class isn't essential to Anglicise,
more an attempt to dehumanise.
By their absurd obsession with caste,
the British reveal a lack of 'class'.

WHEN WE'RE APART

When we're apart I find I'm imprisoned
by a tyrant clock, a dictator of days,
in league with even the crowing cock,
who tortures me with hour long seconds,
and holds me helpless in its hands
and bruises my brain by beating blunt instruments
(the repetitive rhythms of the passage of time).
The worse by far is when I awake,
on the order of an arrogant alarm,
to solitary thought, from sleep's slight respite,
to be reminded, with ticking torment,
of the heartache that's happened since you left,
and the empty pillow where your head has lain.
Then you return, and I that terrible clock disdain.

FROM ABROAD

In the northern hemisphere, winter is about to resume;
back home the wattle trees will be beginning to bloom,
blazing in the bush like yellow galaxies of stars;
new growth will tinge the gum trees red when viewed from afar.
The waratah will be wearing its crimson spring costume,
its stalk towering high, thick and stiff as a broom.
The sugar-cane should now be well over shoulder height,
the fields succulent with syrup and rippling in sunlight.
Hibernating snakes will be beginning to stir,
high country wallabies will be shedding their winter fur.
Whip-birds will be replying to their new-found mates,
their calls echoing and ringing in constant debate.
On homesteads from the coast to the tablelands,
farmers will be looking for new calves to brand.
In the tropical north, humidity will be on the rise;
at Byron Bay surfers paddling out to greet the sunrise.
As trawlers set off to fish the Great Australian Bight,
the sea will be glistening in the clear moonlight.
Here it is bleak and the barometer is falling
but, if I listen hard, I can hear kookaburras calling.

HERE'S TO THE ARBITERS

Here's to the arbiters of public taste!
A toast to those who tell us what to think
about what people are wearing, the wine we drink;
from films to the flavour of toothpaste.
Here's to the columnists and those who critique,
who take it upon themselves to determine
what is pedestrian, passé or chic –
who analyse the issues of our time for us
until we accept the topics they choose to discuss
as the only matters of importance.
A toast to those taking a high moral stand
while cushioned by salaries of a hundred grand!
While most of us cope with our daily grind
they save us from making up our own minds.

THE DREAM

My lately deceased father
came to me in a dream:
the most hideous sight
I have ever seen.
Direct from the grave
he appeared to have come,
his sudden presence struck me dumb –
half decomposed and dripping
flesh, with sightless
sockets and decaying breath.
Through months of remorse
filled, fitful nights I had
mourned my father's death;
brooding on what I
wished I'd said,
while helplessly watching
him gasping for life
as he lay on his hospital bed.
Words that might have
gently soothed the mutually
inflicted and still weeping
sores where we rubbed each
other the wrong way;
seeing in his ceasing to be
my own inevitable mortality;
yet unable to accept the finality
of his predestined demise.
Now he stood before me
in some dreadful disguise.

I began to gabble and, in
my distress, confessed my
feelings and all the affection
I'd failed to express.
The phantom listened: then,
with a satisfied, sepulchral
sigh, the presence left.
And peace of mind prevailed.

THE DEMON DOG

One wild windswept winter's night
when rain lashed the land with Arctic spite,
as I headed home towards Bungay
at the weary end of a working day,
I saw Black Shuck the Demon Dog
padding through the swirling fog.
Moodily emerging from its lair
was a calf-sized dog with shaggy hair,
and saucer-sized red weeping eyes,
and fangs that slashed the air like knives.
It was Black Shuck the Demon Dog
with his icy, putrid breath.
Black Shuck the Demon Dog
who is said to warn of death.
Terrified by what I'd spied,
over the boggy fields I fled,
dreading the evil Demon Dog
would be snapping at my heels.
Soon Bungay's lights drew into sight
and, summoning courage to confront its stare,
I turned to face the horrid hound –
only to find there was nothing there,
except sleet and wind howling
on the tortured air –
no Black Shuck, the Demon Dog,
with his icy putrid breath,
no Black Shuck the Demon Dog,
who is said to warn of death.
I told my wife, my neighbours too,
of the sight I had seen in the gale,

but they just laughed and suggested
I give up Friday nights on the ale.
'There's no such thing as a demon dog
with cold decaying breath.
No such thing as a demon dog
who is said to warn of death'.
I caught a chill, or a chill caught me,
but the doctor said, ' Don't worry!
Your chill was caught by getting drenched.
It's nothing to do with any demon dog.
That's only silly superstition!'
Within a few hours I felt a fever.
It hit me with the force
of a butcher's cleaver.
'I don't understand', the doctor said
and, taking my temperature,
he confined me to bed.
Now lying here helpless,
I'm cursing my luck,
for the legend is true –
the hell hound has struck!
My muscles are aching,
I'm shivering all over
and, though I know I'm stone-
cold-sober, in the room's far
corner I'm sure I can see –
patiently drooling – dear God!
Its eyes are fixed on me!
Black Shuck, the Devil's Dog,
who is said to warn of death.

SUMMER

In summer, the lifestyle where I live
is a light-hearted song celebrating youth.
Composed of fun, sun, surf and sand
it is played on the sweltering FM band
that provides the back-beat to the heat.
Summer smells of suntan lotions,
hamburgers, hotdogs and frying chips,
it is the season when the Sensible
apply sunscreen to dry, chapped lips.
Others spend summer lying belly down
with the bite of the sun on their backs,
slowly cooking in coconut oil, their
gleaming skins turning into hide;
their topless torsos littering the beach
while Adonis designed adolescent boys
wax their boards before braving
the ocean swells or, ignoring the signs
requesting they bathe between the flags,
bodysurf the farthest breakers,
oblivious to the dangers of being
sucked out to sea and drowned
by insidious, unseen undertows …
But when the winds of winter blow
and rattle the shutters on the shops,
the ice-cream vendors all leave town
and all the seasonal stalls shut down,
and abandoned to the corrosive air
the beach, despite being aesthetically
attractive beyond compare, becomes a barren place.

And, gazing over the deserted dunes,
a feeling of emptiness wells up inside,
as if something special, or someone
close to me had died and, momentarily,
the off-shore buoy's bell has a hollow
ring – then I look forward to the first
hint of spring, to when the tourists return,
bringing laughter and summer (though,
regretfully, not mine), back again.

THREE TREES

Three sons sailed across the sea,
three sons sailed for Gallipoli
but the ships returned without them.

To help heal the pain of their tragedy
their parents planted three bunya pine
trees in memory of their sons.

In time, the parents died from old age
broken hearts and sorrow,
but the pine trees continued to grow.

Their tall tips became local landmarks
but, generations later, people forgot
they were planted to honour patriots

with soliloquies, pride and respect –
and in the early twenty-first century
property developers cut down the trees.

THE PAST IS A MUSTY PLACE

The past is a musty place:
a room cluttered with memorabilia,
reminiscences and reminders of yesterday's
pleasures, sorrows and regrets,
youth, innocence and outstanding debts,
on which curtains of dust-laden lace are drawn
to prevent the pictures on the walls from fading.
The past is a procession which has passed:
the footsteps of its participants
still echoing in memory's empty streets,
like musical notes lingering in the ear.
If you live looking back, don't wonder
why the future always passes you by.

I HAVE BEEN TO THE COAL-FACE

I have been to the coal-face,
been at the cutting edge;
stood high above the precipice,
stood wind-swept upon a rocky ledge.
I've seen the mess that vandals make,
felt as if my heart might break,
and now I've seen what angels see.
'But what', asked Saint Michael, 'did you learn,
during your brief moment in eternity?'
'I saw, as far as my eyes enabled me,
that only one thing truly matters
throughout immense infinity.
The simple act of giving,
whether love, hope or charity.'

AS A YOUNG MAN

As a young man I wanted to go places,
and I did; capital cities exposed
their private parts to my prying eyes:
the Parthenon and the Louvre and
the back lanes of Bankside among them.
But now, instead of feeling I've arrived,
I have a sense of being in limbo,
as if in mid-flight on an aircraft,
or on a missile poised at the apex of its trajectory;
neither here nor there but in transit,
suspended somewhere between birth
and the sleep that has no awakening,
hoping reaching my destination will be delayed,
knowing gravity will be obeyed.

WITHOUT THOSE PREPARED TO SPECULATE

Without those prepared to speculate
there will never be a Shangri-La or future
when Homo Sapiens wander from star to star.
For those who suppose and postulate,
who, prepared to risk their dream's destruction,
put themselves to the acid test
and, by facing up to their personal failings,
learn to count themselves among the best.
Those who never dare aspire
never gauge the nature of their fettle,
un-tempered by the forge and fire
they weaken the structure of their metal.
Many may ultimately come to rue
dreams lost forever, that might have come true.

CROSSING THE BAR

Crossing the bar can be dangerous.
The mouth of the Tweed river is renowned;
silted shallow it is considered suicide
to attempt the entrance on an ebbing tide;
the list of boats lost there is lengthy.
Before the railway was built and trucks
ruled the roads, schooners and ketches
brought in supplies and settlers
and carried out the 'red gold' or cedar.
Now the loggers are gone and passengers
fly over the bones of those drowned
when their ships capsized on the bar.
Due to official indifference,
lives continue to be lost today
as consecutive governments baulk
at the cost of dredging; there are
minimal votes to be found among
skeletons sifting sand, and the
trawling fleet's numbers have halved
as they seek safer harbours elsewhere.
But we bought a boat not knowing!
To us, it was the finest dinghy afloat
and we realised the bar – and our
apprehensions – would have to be overcome
or we would always be confined
to the sheltered waters of the river
and catch fewer fish than offshore;
for the fish in the river are scanty,
depleted by professionals permitted
to net a long way upstream and around

the gnarled roots of the mangroves,
the spawning waters for diverse species.
Last, but not least, we decided to dare,
because – like the moon or Mount Everest –
the bar should be crossed because it is there.
'You'll never do it!' the Jonahs sneered.
'Why bother?' our friends and neighbours declared.
'Stay at home and watch TV.
I know where I would rather be!'
We studied charts of shoals and currents;
familiarised ourselves with emergency flares
and took our chance one morning,
when the weather report was 'fair'.
We were promised a light afternoon breeze
and an in-coming under our waterline,
and, as dawn delineated the
foliage of the motionless trees,
we cleaved the river's calm surface
in conditions perfect to water-ski.
Approaching the bar, the boat
began to pitch and roll;
what the day had in store for us
neither could foretell …
We stared in silence, sombrely,
awed by the surge of the restless sea,
impressed by the constant collisions
as waves butted and rebounded
from the breakwaters like medieval
battering rams threatening the
cyclopean walls with brutal demolition.
Exchanging reassuring glances,
we checked our gear was safely stowed
and that the oars were available
and ready, in case we were forced to row.
The sun leapt over the horizon,
a blaze of brightness in the east and,

after tightening the straps of our lifejackets
(and hoping we wouldn't have regrets),
we opened the throttle and surged forward
in search of a Piscean feast.
Steadying the bow into the breakers,
we rose on the first of the
white-capped crests and precariously
balanced there for what felt like forever,
holding our breath in case
the surf's stupendous strength tilted
the boat backwards, length over length,
and, for an instant, we feared we were
about to meet our maker, 'face to face',
wrapped in kelp, in a briny embrace.
But the boat responded, as if alive,
and slid off the wave's shoulder
and into the trough on the sea-ward side;
seconds later we repeated the ride.
Twice more and the waves flattened
ahead of us – the bar had been crossed!
Tension released, we laughed
and cheered in relief and delight,
then, having crossed it once, we
swung our craft about and,
tempting Neptune's notorious spite
(to prove it hadn't been a fluke),
we retraced our hazardous route
and crossed the defeated bar again
before heading out over the sunny sea
for the forty fathom line, where the
biggest fish were supposed to be.

AND THEN THERE IS NOTHING

And then there is nothing;
nothing but the beauty of being.
Once the soul has been seared
and peace made with past mistakes
and regrets, and lost loves and
relationships are remembered with
pleasure at having experienced them:
when unachieved aspirations are seen
not as unconquered summits
but as gently inclining slopes
that will be walked when and if
fortune and fate permit,
then there is nothing but being,
and the serenity simply being brings.

ONCE WHEN THE BUFFETING

Once when the buffeting of baleful winds
made maelstrom among my most cherished beliefs,
with the ease of a breeze bent hopes to griefs,
I clung to what I could, would not rescind.
Now with the knowledge of numbered years
I'll not answer such summons to suffering.
What harm to him can change of wind bring
who learns to let go of what he holds dear?
Even summer, the sceptered season,
whose reign is begun in a glory of green,
all too soon loses its sheen.
Where here hides rhyme or reason?
Like a leaf adrift in a scudding sky
wherever the wind blows there blow I.

NEMESIS

Look over your shoulder, if you dare;
to your horror, one day, I will be there.
In car-parks, at parties and poorly lit zones,
whenever you can, avoid being alone
and, if your life becomes filled with dread,
remember those you lied to and misled
and do what you can to atone;
from now on your life is on loan:
for, like a creature from the living dead,
I am your nemesis waiting up ahead.

'I HAVE WASTED MY LIFE ...'

'I have wasted my life',
the American poet James Wright
wrote in his poem titled
'Lying in a hammock at William Duffy's
farm in Pine Island, Minnesota'.
Don't we all? Whether
writer, wrangler or snake-handler,
don't we all have to choose how
we fritter our days away?

TOLERANCE

You can be a free radical
on a permanent sabbatical
as far as I am concerned.
It doesn't affect me
if you are a 'wannabe',
a nihilist or on the game,
I have no sense of shame.
Therefore I will ignore
any attempt to defile my name.
I have no axe to grind.
It doesn't perturb me
if you are sexist or unkind.
I couldn't care less what
you wear or what colour
you dye your hair – or
if you stick rings through your nose
or your private parts expose.
Just don't pee on my potplants
and we will get along fine.

WHEN NOTHING IS GOING AS PLANNED

When nothing is going as planned,
and good intent is greeted with slow hand claps
and projects are dogged by mishaps
until every idea appears damned;
when business deals meet with catastrophe
and schemes, like rampant threads
unravel and fall apart at the seams
and I find myself a victim of calumny
and my self-esteem is at a discount
and my spirits sink lower than the Dead Sea
and I find myself avoiding company
and thoughts of quitting are paramount;
I remind myself my role is to strive,
but not necessarily to arrive ...

UNANSWERED QUESTIONS

Tell me how, my deceased school friend,
how you came to your untimely end?
Why was such a sensitive soul
selected to meet a premature death
so far from our childhood playground,
muddy Dumaresq Creek's reed-lined shores?

Though I was half a world away,
when news reached me I could clearly
see the entire, awful tragedy;
abandoning the stricken trawler;
your life-raft swamped by the surging sea,
capsizing, spilling you – and your
shipmates – floundering in the frigid water.

I imagined you clinging to a broken oar,
as useful as a floating straw ...

Tell me how, my dear dead friend,
how you came to you untimely end?
What was it attracted a land-lover
like you to the unpredictable sea?
That you, who hitch-hiked and,
footsore, walked from France to Persia,
then ruled by a doomed Shah;
who visited Tibet and crossed India
buoyed by esoteric teachings,
should have drowned, alone in the
night, in the rain and the sea,
is incongruous and unsettling to me ...

Tell me how, my dear friend,
how you came to your untimely end?
Did you curse angrily before you sank
or quietly yield to your fate before you drank?
Did you take to life on the Tasman Sea
to escape from an intolerant society?
Did a shy Hindu find solace among
a fishing boat's accepting crew?
Did I mention how much I miss you?

YOU DON'T NEED
TO BE AVARICIOUS

You don't need to be avaricious to make money,
and Capitalism should heed that it doesn't
need to damage or destroy the ecology:
the air we breath is sacrosanct.
Who dares defile and desecrate the temple?
A compromise has to be found;
for without the allure of affluence
and its subsequent generation of wealth,
we all become poorer in pocket and,
ultimately, it affects a nation's economic health.
A religion dies when it can't find disciples,
and civilization is a thin veneer
upon layer and layer of anarchy and fear.
Appreciate it while it is here.

SOUL FOOD

When the future looks bleak we often
seek a balm for our apprehension.
When fortune frowns and we are down
on our luck, and getting out of bed

takes effort and pluck, we find comfort
with our personal choice of soul food.
Some simply eat fudge and brood;
some choose to numb their dejection

with alcohol or drugs and become bitter,
begrudging others their contentment.
A few, introspectively, turn to poetry
and, on reading, hear voices …

Some are here with us today,
but many belong to writers long dead,
who speak to us as if still alive –
voices conquering and calling across time,

expressing thoughts and emotions
about situations similar to our own,
and the realisation gradually dawns:
someone else has felt the same way!

And with a shiver of recognition
we understand we are not alone,
isolated, in a kind of twilight zone,
but one with the whole of humanity.

FULFILMENT IS FOUND

Fulfilment is found in many forms:
some are not satisfied unless the labels
on what they are wearing are the 'best';
meaning the most fashionable or expensive.
Some are not satisfied unless their house
is the grandest, its position prime.
Many are dissatisfied unless they are
the fastest, the richest or most powerful;
but, except for a fortunate few,
not everyone can be first at what they do.
Most have to be content with being second;
some have a different set of values.
A gardener can be satisfied watching plants grow,
a musician by producing perfect notes on an oboe.

THE FLOWERS THAT
GRACE MY DESK ARE DYING

The flowers that grace my desk are dying.
Listen to the stamen's muted pain
that melts and mews up the stem,
medulla to the blossom's brain.

The flowers that grace my desk are dying.
They droop and rattle like a question
dredging answers in Death's throat
and choke on dumb replies.

The flowers that grace my desk are dying.
Smell the compost on my breath,
there in the flowers stems my spine,
buds my womb, leafs my limb.

EARLY ON A LILAC-LATHERED MORNING

Early on a lilac-lathered morning
clouds, like bursts of shaving foam,
flit across a star-stubbled sky
while a left-over sliver of last
night's moon remains suspended,
like a sleepy all-seeing eye.
In the dawn light, snails' trails shine
and, dripping dew, cobwebs are draped
between the drooping limbs of trees,
their spider-spinners regarding
their victims' plight with indifference
worthy of Judas in the Garden of Gethsemane.
All these wonders offer testimony
to the presence of a mysterious divinity.

SAN ANDREAS THOUGHT

En route to the southern city of San Diego,
in sunny California, a short while ago,
I sought refuge from the Christmas hard sell
in the Sculptors' Garden at Stanford University,
Palo Alto – also home to a nuclear particle accelerator.
There, I found tranquillity and, on public display,
Auguste Rodin's enormous, bronze cast
masterpiece, 'The Gates of Hell'.
Flanked by a muscular Adam and embarrassed Eve,
I stared up at the renowned seated nude male figure,
referred to as 'The Thinker', musing above the Damned,
depicted in agony and woe as they fell from grace.

Only the desultory droning of aircraft on high
and the crunching tread of an occasional passerby's
shoes on the gravel disturbed my reverie.
Nearby cypress pines poked like accusing
fingers into the pristine, cold, clear blue sky;
parking meters dutifully collected coins
and distant trucks rumbled ominously by
as construction workers went about their business.

Some faculty buildings were still being rebuilt
in the wake of the region's last major earthquake,
nearly a decade ago, and standing there,
spell bound, on the San Andreas Fault,
I was visited by the thought that, although all
the efforts of humanity could be considered transitory
and puny before the omnipotence of Nature,
we have the capacity to create Hell here on Earth.

PAYING HOMAGE TO A WELL-KNOWN POET

Paying homage to a well-known poet,
I rang his front doorbell and found him
aged seventy-five but active, erudite,
perceptive, his mind mercurially alive;
his only disability being, he was totally blind.

Unable to see the food scraps on the floor
he welcomed me with polite gentility
before proceeding to discuss the possibility
Bacon and Shakespeare were the same;
that Byron and his half-sister were without blame.

Running a hand vainly through his long, lank,
grey hair and, using the mantle-piece to guide him,
he groped to his favourite armchair and sat
– a modern Homer – beside the telephone,
oblivious to the squalor that was his home;
unaware the armrests were grimy with grease;
that, had his kitchen been open to the public,
a health inspector would have closed it.

Being a good guest I accepted the coffee
he offered and swallowed, hoping I wouldn't gag.
Unlike lucky Milton, he didn't have daughters
dedicated to his care and collating the verses
he composed while sitting on his garden swing
or a fag but, this President of the Society,
winner of the Gold Medal for Poetry,
wasn't perturbed or worried in the slightest!

Shirt tale hanging out of his dirty jeans,
his pullover stained with tannin and caffeine,
face cadaverous, his teeth rotten, blackened
stumps and surrounded by stench and decay,
he chatted on cheerfully, like the tutor he once was,
about wasps, wildflowers, basil and Boz,
constantly distinguishing knowledge from hearsay,
determined not to waste a precious moment of the day.
His conversation ignored his predicament
and his inquiring voice might have belonged
to an eager student, replete with intellectual curiosity,
storing information in his brain's repository
in the lead-up to a major examination.

His speech was like listening to lines of his verse
and, like his poems, concerned with life.
His words floated between us, soap bubbles
in mid-air, clean, bright, filled with hope,
without a hint of depression or despair ...

Before me sat a scholar about to go on holiday,
not a husk of a man close to his Doomsday.

I NO LONGER DREAM

I no longer dream in time I might
reach rainbows, discover mountains
capped in white delight; no more
those dreams of races won, of inventing
perpetual summer suns; instead,
these mornings when pipes burst and break,
and frost licks the lawn as far as the garden gate,
I seek those patches, those few corners
of the yard where, blessed and bright,
in Winter's weak sunlight, I sit and bask
in pleasures of the heart – and dream.
And dream I'll be remembered; not for deeds
or fame, but as someone who saw their pain
as passing clouds bringing summer rain.

THE PEACHEY STONE

'There is a spot in the churchyard, near the footpath, on the brow
of the hill looking towards Windsor, and a tomb under a large tree,
where I used to sit for hours and hours when a boy. This was my
favourite spot.'

Excerpt from a letter written by Lord Byron in Italy, 1822.

It is high on Harrow-on-the-Hill:
you don't have to search for
the spire of St. Mary's Church,
it is a landmark, like the statue of Christ
that towers over Rio in Brazil.

Dainty, wandering, dandelion seeds
float on the sultry evening air,
mingling with echoes of massed prayer;
like overjoyed prisoners gratefully freed,
they cavort and dart at different speeds.

Another free spirit often came here –
especially on days that were crystal clear –
resting his distorted and still growing
bones on a weather worn tombstone,
surveying this spectacle, he forever held dear.

Byron adored this panoramic view and,
as a child, frequently sat here on his own,
upon this now famous 'Peachey Stone';
seeking relief from his cramped scholastic pew,
escaping ridicule about his built-up shoe.

Unaware of impending immortality,
he found respite from pedants' rule
in this churchyard near his school;
his thoughts, perhaps, on odes and spondees,
preferring his own company.

Although more urban and less green
(having lost legions of oak and yew)
the pleasant aspect Byron once knew
still remains far from routine –
it is an impressive, uplifting scene.

'The mountains look on Marathon –
and Marathon looks on the sea ...'

The child's eyes looking from this hill
were adult eyes at Marathon,
a brief lifetime further on.
did this prospect help instil
a delight and reverence for free will?

Gazing out over the Thames Valley,
Did the boy Byron foresee himself
opposing tyranny? Was a youth
inspired by dancing seeds to give all
for freedom and, if necessary, bleed?

SYMMACHUS THE PAGAN

Symmachus the pagan appealed to the Emperor:
'We look at the same stars; the sky belongs
to all; the same universe surrounds us. Does
it matter by which method each seeks the truth?
One cannot arrive at so sublime a secret by only one road.'
Bishop Ambrose responded to the pagan's appeal:
'What you do not know, we know from the word of God;
what you seek, we have established as truth from the
very wisdom of God … Your ways do not agree with ours.'
Within a decade Theodosius issued his edict to close
the temples saying: 'Burn all books hostile to Christianity
lest they cause anger and scandalize the pious!'
And, as black clad monks destroyed shrines and scrolls,
intolerance became ascendant, entrenched and holy.

LIKE POMPEIIENS PRAYING

Like Pompeiiens praying for Jove's protection
while watching Vesuvius' pyroclastic clouds
hurtling towards them and their incineration;
like King Cunute ordering the tide to recede,
those who believe humanity can avoid
an increase in global warming or prevent
an ice-age are like primitives practising
sympathetic magic in an attempt to appease
awesome primeval forces. Nature is neutral,
favouring neither hubristic humans or cockroaches,
nor rod-like and still evolving bacilli.
Nature is implacable and does not care whether
the planet heats or freezes or what mix of protons
and nuclei slithers forth from its elemental dust.

IF YOU FEEL SOMEONE

If you feel someone is pointing a bone
and you want to be or find yourself alone,
go to the town of Alice Springs –
it is easily reached on alloy wings.
The Central Australian night sky
will provide you with a perfect alibi
if you decide not to return.
For the stars out there don't merely shine,
they burn brighter than a water buffalo's luminous green
eyes
or lasers at the bottom of some Stygian mine.
Meet a mystical Min Min light
where the meteorites look like fireworks at night
and, staring out into the infinite cosmos,
spiral nebulas share any sense of loss.

THE POET

There will be no pause at his passing.
The state won't send him on his way
with a public holiday or order
monuments in his memory.

His demise won't be noted in the media.
No-one will write his obituary,
deliver a lengthy eulogy at a
well attended funeral ceremony.

Politicians won't decorate his cortege;
no minister, magnate or magistrate
will dirty their shoes in his wake;
there will be few wreaths to remember him.

There will be no one minute silence.
No flags fluttering at half mast
while mourners dutifully reflect upon
some momentous accomplishment past.

There were none. He did not make
a name waging war, like some
warrior knight in days of yore
or find financial reward in the city.

Nor did he spend his waking hours
in the so-called public service
or aspire to forge a fortune in futures.
He had no desire to set the world on fire.

For while the movers and the shakers,
the empire builders and their breakers,
were busy with their bricks and mortar,
he was more interested in their daughters.

Refusing to be led like a lamb to slaughter,
he turned away from the dealers in dollars
who went to work in ties and collars
and wore open toed sandals instead.

He couldn't become an industrial tycoon,
publicising his name on the side
of some promotional blimp or balloon,
he found such aspirations facile,

and began a quest of a different style.
Not for him the blind pursuit
of transitory success and fame,
he decided to pursue a different game.

Beguiled by the beauty of the beast
he sought the knowledge of the heart and,
in the process of devouring Nature's feast,
found fabulous wealth where wealth was least.

For, if assailed by Winter's cold,
sunlight is more valuable than gold
and the lost sailor is rich with delight
beneath the diamonds of a star filled night.

So leaping off the intellectual fence,
and ignoring physics and biochemistry,
he started to search for the essence
of his inner-being and psyche.

Like the early Gnostic scholars,

he studied the secrets of the soul
and discovered hidden treasures
disdained by those seeking worldly pleasures.

And during that protracted search
through his inner, angst-ridden Id,
he found contentment in existing
shone brightest through all he thought or did.

Yet any captain of industry – or other
upholder of temporal and secular
authority – would have considered him
to be an apathetic under-achiever.

But the poet saw infinity in an hour and
the purpose of being in ephemeral flowers;
he saw the human spirit is unique,
sometimes pure, more often weak.

He saw that rain refreshes the earth;
that what is lost can be found;
that seeds are encouraged to germinate
by the fire that scorches the ground:

that when we laugh at our own despair,
we sow hope into the air; for we are made
of wind and sky and live forever in our
loved ones' hearts, even after we die.

SIC TRANSIT GLORIA MUNDI

Time is termite devouring my days,
denying me longevity and repeatedly
telling me, eventually, nothing
can save me from ceasing to be.
Time is a mirror in which I see
my wrinkles constantly reminding me
of my transitory grip on existence.
Mornings merge into afternoons,
my days are measured in coffee spoons
and summer soon turns into winter.
So faced with anno domini,
I watch the kites wheel in the sky,
trying to imprint the image on my mind
as if storing it for recall after I die.

IT GETS HARDER

It gets harder to be positive
as you get older; the negatives,
like arthritis and rheumatism,
creep closer, skulking thieves
casing your house and waiting
for you to walk out the door.
Concerns about medical insurance
and superannuation replace the parties
and devil-may-care attitude of before.
Bypasses become more pertinent
than crossroads, and favourite
photos of once familiar faces
remind of moments momentarily
frozen in time, vaguely remembered
tableaux in a half forgotten mime.

EVERY END HAS
ITS BEGINNING

Every end has its beginning:
but often it is difficult to determine
where beginnings end and ends begin;
transitions are nebulous by nature.
Conception is a kind of beginning;
death is life's logical end;
yet death is often seen as temporary,
a stage after which is experienced
a better, more blissful state of being.
But if death is definitive,
lives spent anticipating are squandered,
and life should be lived for the moment.
Until there is an ultimate end,
let there be numerous new beginnings.